BEARS

LIFE IN THE WILD

by Monica Kulling
illustrated by Jean Cassels

The Grizzly bear sniffs the air.
She smells danger!

Dear Parent:

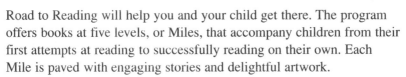

Buckle up! You are about to join your child on a very exciting journey. The destination? Independent reading!

Road to Reading will help you and your child get there. The program offers books at five levels, or Miles, that accompany children from their first attempts at reading to successfully reading on their own. Each Mile is paved with engaging stories and delightful artwork.

Getting Started
For children who know the alphabet and are eager to begin reading
• easy words • fun rhythms • big type • picture clues

Reading With Help
For children who recognize some words and sound out others with help
• short sentences • pattern stories • simple plotlines

Reading On Your Own
For children who are ready to read easy stories by themselves
• longer sentences • more complex plotlines • easy dialogue

First Chapter Books
For children who want to take the plunge into chapter books
• bite-size chapters • short paragraphs • full-color art

Chapter Books
For children who are comfortable reading independently
• longer chapters • occasional black-and-white illustrations

There's no need to hurry through the Miles. Road to Reading is designed without age or grade levels. Children can progress at their own speed, developing confidence and pride in their reading ability no matter what their age or grade.

So sit back and enjoy the ride—every Mile of the way!

For Miriam, who loves animals
M.K.

To three wonderful
men in my life:
Craig, Michael, and John
J.C.

Library of Congress Cataloging-in-Publication Data
Kulling, Monica.
Bears : life in the wild / by Monica Kulling ; illustrated by Jean Cassels.
  p. cm. — (Road to reading. Mile 3)
Summary: Provides facts about bears, from grizzly and polar bears to more exotic
species like the sloth bear and the spectacled bear.
ISBN 0-307-26303-7 (pbk.)
1. Bears—Juvenile literature. [1. Bears.] I. Cassels, Jean, ill.
II. Title. III. Series.
QL737.C27K85 1998
599.78—dc21   98-12022
                                                               CIP
                                                               AC

A GOLDEN BOOK • New York
Golden Books Publishing Company, Inc. New York, New York 10106

ISBN: 0-307-26303-7

A MCMXCVIII

Nearby her twin cubs
are playing in the summer sun.
She will fight to the death
to protect them.

On the Alaskan trail,

two hikers come around the bend.

The mother Grizzly goes into action.

She rears up on her hind legs.

She lets out an earth-shaking ROAR!

What should the hikers do?

Should they run?

NO!

The Grizzly would catch them.

A Grizzly can move faster

than a freight train!

Should they fight?

NO!

The Grizzly would crush them.
A Grizzly has huge muscles
in its shoulders that make
its front legs very powerful.
It also has six-inch claws
and a mighty jaw.

Should the hikers back off slowly?
YES!
If the bear attacks,
they should lie on the ground
and play dead.
That way the bear will think
they are harmless.

But the Grizzly does not attack.
She sees that the hikers
are not going to hurt her cubs.
She lets the hikers go.

Bears are timid animals.
They do not go looking
for people to attack.
But if you surprise a bear,
or get too near its young,
WATCH OUT!

There are eight species
of bears in the world.
Three species live
in North America.
They are the Brown bear,
the Black bear,
and the Polar bear.

The Grizzly is a Brown bear.
Because it is so fast
and so strong,
it is the most feared bear
in the world.

But a baby Grizzly
is not scary at all.
When it is born,
a Grizzly is much smaller
than a human baby.
It weighs only
a pound and a half—
about the same as a grapefruit!

At first, the Grizzly cub
stays close to its mother.
She protects the cub
from enemies—
including its own father!
A male Grizzly will eat his cub
if he gets the chance.

After two and a half years,

the Grizzly cub is full-grown.

It weighs 700 pounds.

It is just as scary

as its mother and father!

The Black bear is known
as a friendly bear.
Black bears are often
spotted in parks.
Some get so used to people
that they beg for food!
In some ways,
Black bears are like us.
They can walk on their back legs.
They are smart and curious.

And they love sweets—
especially honey!

In 1902, a Black bear cub
visited the White House!
President Theodore Roosevelt,
who was also called Teddy,
found the cub on a hunting trip.
Cartoonists loved to draw pictures
of the President with his bear.

That gave a toymaker
named Morris Michtom an idea.
He made a stuffed bear
and asked the President
if he could name it after him.
The President said yes—
and the Teddy Bear was born!

Black bears are not always black.
Some are cinnamon brown,
or beige, or even white.
These *white* Black bears
live in British Columbia.
They are sometimes called
"ghost bears."

Grizzly bears and Black bears
both live in parts of North America
where winters are cold.
Most Grizzly bears live
in the western mountains.
Most Black bears live
in the northern woods.

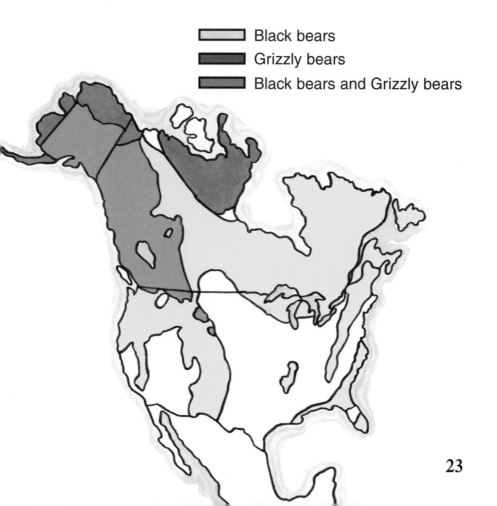

- Black bears
- Grizzly bears
- Black bears and Grizzly bears

When the days get short,

these bears know that soon

food will be scarce.

There will be no fish to catch

or berries to find.

24

The bears begin to eat and eat—
up to 20 hours a day!
They add six inches of fat
to their bodies.
They will live off this fat
through the long winter.

After the first snowfall,
each bear makes a den.
This Black bear is digging a cave
under a tree.
The roots will keep the roof
from caving in.

The bear lines his den
with dried grass and leaves
to make it warm.
Then he curls up inside
and goes to sleep.

All through the winter,
the bear sleeps.
His body makes its own water
so he doesn't need to drink.
His body also recycles waste.
That means he doesn't have to
go to the bathroom—
for up to seven months!

In the spring,

the bear wakes up.

He is hungry!

The first thing he does

is look for food.

These crickets

will make a tasty snack.

Polar bears live
in the coldest spot
on earth—
the Arctic Circle.
But they do not sleep
through the winter.
Why not?

All year long,
these bears can hunt
their favorite foods—
walruses and seals.

Polar bears are
perfectly made for life
in the ice and snow.
Their white fur hides them
from enemies.
The black skin under the fur
keeps the sun's heat in.
The Polar bear's huge feet
make great paddles
for swimming,
and great snowshoes
for walking on ice.

Polar bears walk
thousands of miles
across the Arctic ice
and never see
another kind of bear.
As far as they know,
they are the only bears on earth!

There are
five other bear species
that do not sleep
through the winter.
They don't have to—
they live in warm places,
where food is always plentiful.

The Spectacled bear
lives in South America.
It gets its name
from the white lines
around its eyes.
It looks as if
it's wearing glasses!

The Asian Black bear
is sometimes called
the "moon bear"
because the shape on its chest
looks like a half-moon.

The Sun bear lives in Malaysia.

It is the world's smallest bear.

It never weighs
more than 100 pounds.

The Sloth bear of India
eats ants and termites.
It has no front teeth!
This bear can use its nose
like a vacuum hose.
That makes it easy
to suck up its dinner!

The Giant Panda
is the rarest bear.
It can only be found
in a very small area of China.
Here it feeds on
tender bamboo shoots.
The Giant Panda must eat
all day just to stay alive!

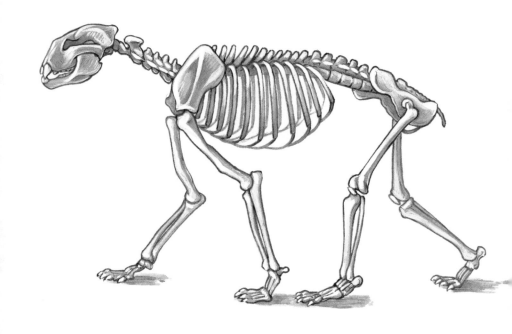

Long ago, there were
more bear species.
There was one species
known as the "bulldog bear."
Its skeleton tells us
that this bear had longer legs
than most bears.
But the bulldog bear
became extinct.

Other species
are in danger of extinction.
The Grizzly is one.
There used to be so many
Grizzly bears in California
that a Grizzly was put
on the state flag.

But as forests were destroyed,
Grizzly bears were pushed out.
Now there is not one Grizzly
left in California.

Today there are parks
set aside for bears
and other wildlife.
There is no hunting.
There is no trapping.
Trees cannot be cut down,
and streams cannot be polluted.
Denali National Park in Alaska
is one such place.

Here, bears can
raise their young
in peace.